W9-BRD-116

Sara Swan Miller

Rabbits, Pikas, and Hares

Franklin Watts - A Division of Scholastic Inc.

New York • Toronto • London • Auckland • Sydney
Mexico City • New Delhi • Hong Kong
Danbury, Connecticut

For my mother,
and the rabbit in your garden

Photographs ©: American Society of Mammalogists, Mammal Images Library: 32, 33 (J. D. Haweeli), 40, 41 (J. Visser); Animals Animals/Maresa Pryor: 35; B. Moose Peterson/WRP: 22, 23; BBC Natural History Unit: 21 (Niall Benvie), 37 (John Cancalosi), 5 bottom left, 5 top left (Brian Lightfoot), cover (Rico & Ruiz), 42 (Lynn Stone); Bruce Coleman: 24, 25 (R. Mittermeir), 31 (Han Reinhard); Corbis-Bettmann/George Lepp: 18, 19; Dembinsky Photo Assoc./John Gerlach: 27; NHPA/G.I. Bernard: 6; Peter Arnold Inc./C. Allan Morgan: 15; Photo Researchers, NY: 39 (G. C. Kelley), 7 (Maslowski), 1 (Rod Planck), 43 (Carroll Seghers); Visuals Unlimited: 13 (Gary W. Carter), 5 top right (John Gerlach), 5 bottom right (Gary Meszaros), 16, 17 (Tom J. Ulrich), 29 (Tom Walker).

Illustrations by Pedro Julio Gonzalez, Steve Savage, and A. Natacha Pimentel C.

The photo on the cover shows a European rabbit. The photo on the title page shows a baby cottontail rabbit.

Library of Congress Cataloging-in-Publication Data

Miller, Sara Swan.
      Rabbits, pikas, and hares / Sara Swan Miller ; [Pedro Julio Gonzalez, Steve Savage, and A. Natacha Pimentel C., illustrators].
            p. cm. — (Animals in order)
      Includes bibliographical references and index.
      ISBN 0-531-11634-4
      1. Lagomorpha—Juvenile literature. [1. Rabbits. 2. Pikas. 3. Hares.] I. Gonzalez, Pedro Julio, ill. II. Savage, Steve, ill. III. Pimentel C., A. Natacha, ill. IV. Title. V. Series.
QL737.L3 M56 2001
599.32—dc21   2001017959

© 2002 Franklin Watts, a Division of Scholastic Inc.
All rights reserved. Published simultaneously in Canada.
Printed in the United States of America.
1 2 3 4 5 6 7 8 9 10 R 11 10 09 08 07 06 05 04 03 02

Contents

What Is a Lagomorph?

Have you ever watched a rabbit as it hops about and nibbles clover? Have you ever seen a hare bounding away from a hungry coyote? Because of their long ears and legs, you may have guessed that rabbits and hares are related. You were right! What you probably didn't know is that they have another relative—the little short-eared, short-legged pika.

In the past, scientists thought that rabbits, pikas, and hares were rodents, like mice and chipmunks. Now scientists know that rabbits, pikas, and hares are closely related. They belong to a group, or *order*, of mammals—the *lagomorphs* (LAG-oh-morfs). They have certain traits in common that rodents don't share.

On the next page, you can see three lagomorphs and one rodent. Can you guess how the rabbit, hare, and pika are different from the muskrat?

4

Brown hare

American pika

European rabbit

Muskrat

Traits of the Lagomorphs

The most important difference between lagomorphs and rodents is hard to see without looking into their mouths. Both have a pair of *incisors* in the front of their jaws, then a gap between the incisors and the *cheek teeth*. But lagomorphs have another pair of small, peglike incisors behind their front pair.

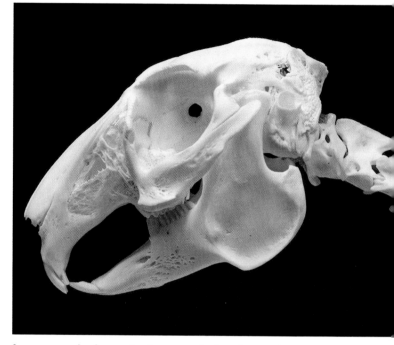

Lagomorphs have incisors and cheek teeth.

Lagomorphs have other traits in common that are easier to see. They have long, soft fur that keeps them warm. They even have fur on the bottom of each foot! Their eyes are set high on the sides of their heads, so they can see danger coming from any direction. Most lagomorphs have longer ears than rodents, and lagomorphs' tails are short and puffy instead of long and thin.

They have other special features. They can close off their nostrils with flaps of skin to keep out dust and water. Other folds of skin on their lips can meet behind their incisors, so they can gnaw with their mouths closed.

All lagomorphs are *herbivores*. They eat only plants—grasses, leaves, bark, and sometimes seeds and roots. They have an unusual way of digesting this plant matter. When they eat, their food comes out the other end as soft pellets. They eat these pellets and digest them again. That way they get more nutrients out of their food. The second set of pellets is hard and dry, and they don't eat them.

There are two *families* of lagomorphs—the hares and rabbits, and the pikas. Do you know the difference between rabbits and hares? Most rabbits make their nests in *burrows* they dig. The babies, called *kittens*, are born blind and naked. Most hares make nests in shallow hollows called *forms*. Their babies, or *leverets*, are born with fur and open eyes. They can hop about soon after birth. Like rabbits, pikas are born blind, naked, and helpless.

Most lagomorphs have several large litters a year. However, only one in ten of the young will survive their first year because they have so many enemies.

All lagomorphs, including this desert cottontail, are herbivores.

The Order of Living Things

A tiger has more in common with a house cat than with a daisy. A true bug is more like a butterfly than a jellyfish. Scientists arrange living things into groups based on how they look and how they act. A tiger and a housecat belong to the same group, but a daisy belongs to a different group.

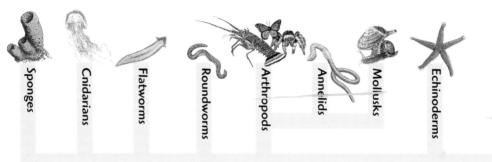

Sponges Cnidarians Flatworms Roundworms Arthropods Annelids Mollusks Echinoderms

Animals

Plants Fungi

Protists

Monerans

All living things can be placed in one of five groups called *kingdoms*: the plant kingdom, the animal kingdom, the fungus kingdom, the moneran kingdom, or the protist kingdom. You can probably name some of the creatures in the plant and animal kingdoms. The fungus kingdom includes mushrooms, yeasts, and molds. The moneran and protist kingdoms contain thousands of living things that are too small to see without a microscope.

8

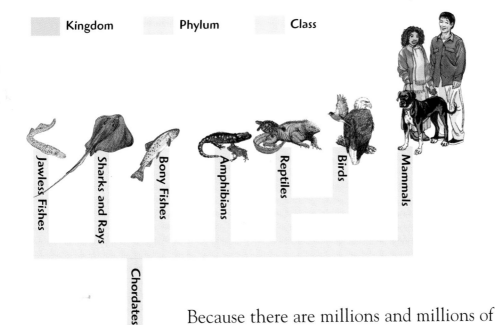

Kingdom   Phylum   Class

Jawless Fishes | Sharks and Rays | Bony Fishes | Amphibians | Reptiles | Birds | Mammals

Chordates

Because there are millions and millions of living things on Earth, some of the members of one kingdom may not seem all that similar. The animal kingdom includes creatures as different as tarantulas and trout, jellyfish and jaguars, salamanders and sparrows, elephants and earthworms.

To show that an elephant is more like a jaguar than an earthworm, scientists further separate the creatures in each kingdom into more specific groups. The animal kingdom can be divided into nine *phyla*. Humans belong to the chordate phylum. All chordates have a backbone.

Each phylum can be subdivided into many *classes*. Humans, mice, and elephants all belong to the mammal class. Each class can be further divided into orders, orders into families, families into *genera*, and genera into *species*. All members of a species are very similar.

9

How Lagomorphs Fit In

You can probably guess that lagomorphs belong to the animal kingdom. They have much more in common with bees and bats than with maple trees and morning glories.

Lagomorphs belong to the chordate phylum. Almost all chordates have a backbone and a skeleton. Can you think of other chordates? Examples include lions, mice, snakes, birds, fish, and whales.

The chordate phylum can be divided into several classes. Lagomorphs belong to the mammal class. A mammal is an animal that has a backbone and feeds its young with mother's milk. Mice, whales, dogs, cats, and humans are all mammals.

There are twenty-eight different orders of mammals. The lagomorphs make up one of these orders. The scientific name for this order means "hare shaped." They all share certain traits, including an extra set of incisors behind their front incisors.

There are about eighty species of lagomorphs. They are native to all continents except Australia and Antarctica. People have introduced them into many new places, so now you're likely to find them almost anywhere. You will learn more about fifteen species of lagomorphs in this book.

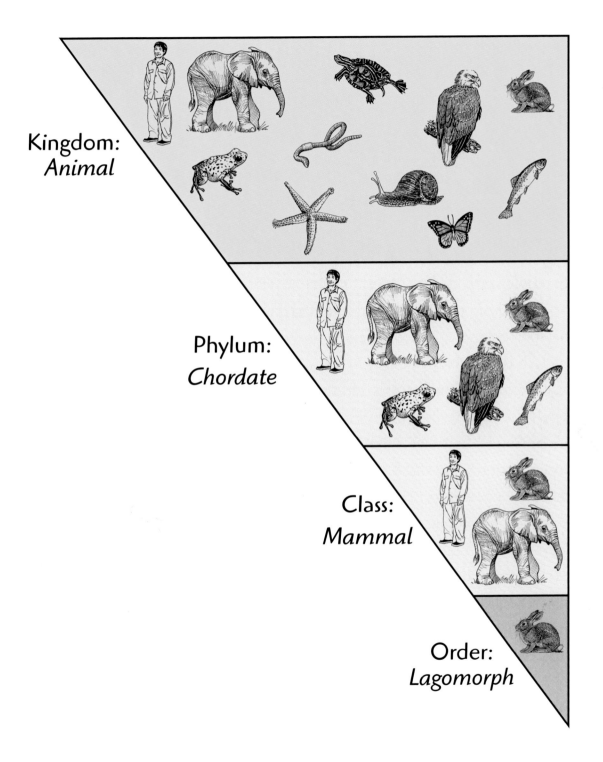

Kingdom:
Animal

Phylum:
Chordate

Class:
Mammal

Order:
Lagomorph

Cottontails

FAMILY: Leporidae
COMMON EXAMPLE: Eastern cottontail
GENUS AND SPECIES: *Sylvilagus floridanus*
SIZE: 15 1/2 to 19 inches (40 to 48 cm)

An eastern cottontail rabbit crouches in the safety of a thicket as it quietly grooms its soft, thick fur. Every so often it sits up on its back legs, looks about, and sniffs the air for danger. All clear! It settles back down to nap away the long daylight hours.

Cottontails come out at dusk to nibble on grass, clover, and wild strawberries. As most gardeners know, they love flowers and vegetables too! In the winter, they survive by eating twigs, bark, and buds.

Spring is their mating season, and eastern cottontails have an interesting mating ritual. A *buck* chases a *doe* until she turns and faces him. She punches at him with her forepaws like a boxer. Then they both crouch down and face each other. Suddenly, one of them leaps straight up in the air. The chase begins again. They repeat this ritual over and over until they finally mate.

Like other rabbits, cottontails have many enemies. They need to have many kittens because not all of them survive. A doe has three or four litters a year with as many as twelve kittens in each. Born blind and naked, the kittens grow quickly. In just 2 weeks they leave the nest. They can have kittens of their own when they're only 3 months old—if they don't get eaten first!

Hares

FAMILY: Leporidae
COMMON EXAMPLE: Brown hare
GENUS AND SPECIES: *Lepus europaeus*
SIZE: 17 1/4 to 30 inches (44 to 76 cm)

Have you ever heard the expression "mad as a March hare"? If you've ever watched brown hares during their mating season in March, you would know where that expression comes from. They seem to go crazy!

The males chase one another across the fields in a mad fight over the females. They leap and kick at one another. They box with their front feet as they grunt and gnash their teeth. When a male is hurt, he lets out a piercing scream. What a wild scene!

When mating season is over, the hares settle down. The does give birth to litters of leverets in a grassy form. A doe only feeds her leverets at night. Soon they leave the nest, and each leveret finds its own safe place to hide. For 4 weeks, the doe comes to visit them one by one. She feeds them with her rich milk. Then they're on their own.

Brown hares have many enemies, including hawks, foxes, and dogs. When a *predator* comes near, a hare freezes. Its heartbeat slows down so its breathing won't give it away. But if its enemy finds it, its heart suddenly speeds up to 3 times its normal beat. It springs from its hiding place and races away to safety.

Pikas

FAMILY: Ochotonidae
COMMON EXAMPLE: American pika
GENUS AND SPECIES: *Ochotona princeps*
SIZE: 6 to 8 1/2 inches (15 to 22 cm)

Why is that pika running off with a bunch of flowers in its mouth? Is it carrying a bouquet? No, but it's behaving in a way that is almost as surprising. It's building a haypile!

Pikas are active throughout the cold winter, when it's hard for them to find fresh grasses and flowers to eat. Storing food in stacks helps them survive the winter, when the only other plants they can find to eat are mosses and lichens.

They begin making their haypiles in late summer. They start stacking grass and weeds on sunny rocks. The piles are as big as a bushel or more, but the little pikas keep moving the piles to sunny places until the grass is dry. Then they store the piles under rock ledges for the winter.

Besides building haypiles, there are other ways that pikas are different from rabbits and hares. Pikas have short, round ears and almost no tail. Their hind legs are not very long, and they run instead of hop.

16

Pikas are much noisier than other lagomorphs too. When a pika spots danger, it barks or whistles loudly. Then it dives for cover among the rocks where it lives. Pikas also defend their *territory* by sharply calling, "Caack!" During the mating season, males sing a song to attract a mate. Both males and females sing at harvest time.

Rabbits

FAMILY: Leporidae
EXAMPLE: Volcano rabbit
GENUS AND SPECIES: *Romerolagus diazi*
SIZE: 10 1/2 to 12 1/4 inches (27 to 31 cm)

The only place to find volcano rabbits is high on the slopes of certain volcanoes about 30 miles (48 km) southeast of Mexico City. These rare creatures live in a small area—about 149 square miles (386 sq km). They prefer to live in pine or alder forests.

Volcano rabbits are little and look more like pikas than rabbits. They have short ears and hardly any tails. They behave like pikas too. Instead of hopping like rabbits, they trot about on their short legs. They also squeak and bark when danger threatens.

During the day, they stay in their burrows. The burrows are a complicated system of tunnels with many exits hidden under clumps of grass. Inside, the rabbits rest together in nests of grass and fur.

At dusk, they come out and run around in the complex runways they have made through the dense clumps of grass. Their favorite food is the young shoots of zacatón grass, which grows only in the small area where they live.

18

Volcano rabbits are endangered. People hunt them and destroy their *habitat* for timber and farming. Cattle and sheep eat the zacatón the rabbits feed on, and people cut it up to make thatch for their roofs. Farmers think of them as pests because the rabbits sometimes eat corn or oats. They shoot the rabbits on sight. Will these rare rabbits survive?

Rabbits

FAMILY: Leporidae
COMMON EXAMPLE: European rabbit
GENUS AND SPECIES: *Oryctolagus cuniculus*
SIZE: 15 to 20 inches (38 to 51 cm)

European rabbits have a much more peaceful mating season than brown hares. If a buck spots a doe, he will chase after her as she zigzags through the meadow. Soon she sits still, and the buck hops over and shows her the white underside of his tail. If she likes him, the two stay close together. They rub their noses together and groom each other's heads. Then they mate.

European rabbits live together in a big burrow underground called a warren. It has a lot of tunnels and rooms with many exits and entrances. A *colony* of about six to ten adult rabbits live in a warren. They have strict rules about who gets to live where and who gets to mate with whom.

The strongest male is the leader. Only he gets to mate with the lead female. He mates with the other females, too, so he is the father of most of the kittens in the colony. The lead female gets to raise her kittens in the main burrow—the safest spot.

The lead male defends the colony's territory by marking it with scent from glands in his cheeks. He sprays the other members with his scent, too, so they have a group smell. He will fiercely attack any intruding males. Strange rabbits, beware!

3 6878 00071 4482

Rabbits

FAMILY: Leporidae
COMMON EXAMPLE: Brush rabbit
GENUS AND SPECIES: *Sylvilagus bachmani*
SIZE: 12 to 14 1/2 inches (30 to 37 cm)

Unlike volcano rabbits, brush rabbits are common. They live in large numbers from northern Oregon to southern California. What is the secret of their survival?

Brush rabbits will eat almost any plant! In the summer they live off different kinds of grasses. They also like foxtails, thistles, and—especially—clover. When they can't find freshly growing greens, they graze on leaves, twigs, buds, berries, and the tender bark of blackberry or rose bushes. They even will eat the roots of poison hemlock. Like other rabbits, they get extra vitamin B by eating their own droppings.

The other secret of their survival is that they know how to hide from predators. They live in dense brush and hardly ever come out into the open. During the day, they sit perfectly still in the brush. No one would guess that they're there. At dusk, they get up to feed and follow tunnels they have made in the undergrowth.

Brush rabbits have a lot of enemies. Besides bobcats, coyotes, foxes, weasels, snakes, and many other predators on the ground, these rabbits have to be on the lookout for hawks and owls that may spot them from the air. If a brush rabbit is somehow discovered in its hiding place, it thumps its back feet in alarm and zigzags swiftly away. Wild predators aren't the only danger. People also hunt these rabbits for their tasty flesh. Yet brush rabbits not only survive, but thrive.

Pikas

FAMILY: Ochotonidae
COMMON EXAMPLE: Royle's pika
GENUS AND SPECIES: *Ochotona roylei*
SIZE: 6 to 8 inches (15 to 20 cm)

Who is singing that sweet song from the rocks? A Royle's pika is sitting on his "singing rock" whistling away. His song doesn't sound so sweet to other male pikas, though. He's sending them a message: "Keep away! This is MY territory!"

Soon his mate and her young poke their noses out of the rocks and blink in the morning sun. They're hungry after a long night in their nests. Together they trot into the meadow to munch on the new grass and weeds sprouting there.

Unlike other pikas, Royle's pikas don't store food in haypiles for the winter. They live in places where there is not much snow, so most of the time they can find enough fresh food. When it does snow, they burrow down to find plants still growing underneath.

Royle's pikas prefer to live in rocky places with meadows nearby where they can find grass and moss to eat. Sometimes they live in forests growing on rocks, and they nest in small caves under the roots.

Once in a while, these pikas make their nests in the rock walls of people's houses. Then they sneak inside to nibble on any bread or baked goods they can find!

Hares

FAMILY: Leporidae
COMMON EXAMPLE: Snowshoe hare
GENUS AND SPECIES: *Lepus americanus*
SIZE: 16 to 20 inches (41 to 51 cm)

It's not hard to guess how the snowshoe hare got its name. Its big feet are covered with thick fur, and its hind feet also have stiff hairs that make them look like snowshoes. The hare's hind feet help it hop about on top of deep snow.

Snowshoe hares live in the northern United States and Canada, and they are well adapted to a life of cool summers and cold, harsh winters. In summer, their coat is rusty brown. It helps them hide in the woods. Their coat gradually turns white during the fall. By winter, they are covered with a warm, thick coat of white fur. If they sit still, a hawk or a lynx may not spot them against the snow.

A snowshoe hare's diet changes with the seasons. In the summer, it has a good food supply—grass, clover, dandelions, and blackberry shoots. In the winter, it gnaws on buds, twigs, and bark with its strong incisors. It even eats pine and spruce needles!

A female snowshoe hare may have as many as four litters a year with up to ten leverets at a time. That's a lot of new snowshoe hares coming into the world! But these lagomorphs have many enemies. Bobcats, coyotes, foxes, weasels, owls, and hawks love a fine meal of snowshoe hare.

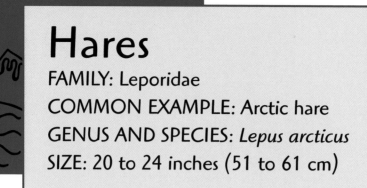

Hares

FAMILY: Leporidae
COMMON EXAMPLE: Arctic hare
GENUS AND SPECIES: *Lepus arcticus*
SIZE: 20 to 24 inches (51 to 61 cm)

Arctic hares live in Canada, Greenland, and arctic islands—where winter winds shriek and the snow is deep. How do they survive?

They have dense underfur and long, thick outer hairs. Their hair keeps them almost as warm as you are when you wear a two-layered down jacket and thermal underwear. Their coats turn white in winter and help them blend in with their surroundings.

An Arctic hare has other ways to keep warm too. It rests on snowdrifts behind boulders that block the wind. When it's really cold, it tucks its feet in tightly and folds its ears snugly down on its back. Only the pads of its hind feet touch the snow. It looks like a furry, white bowling ball.

Sometimes Arctic hares burrow into the snow for warmth. They usually make a pit in the snow to snuggle into, but sometimes they tunnel into snowdrifts and make *dens*. Oddly, though, they don't curl up together for warmth. They live alone most of the time.

It's hard for Arctic hares to find food in winter, but they have special tools. They have long, strong claws that dig through hard-packed snow and extra-long incisors that help them gnaw on moss and lichen. Arctic hares are real survivors!

Hares

FAMILY: Leporidae
COMMON EXAMPLE: Mountain hare
GENUS AND SPECIES: *Lepus timidus*
SIZE: 16 1/2 to 24 inches (42 to 61 cm)

Brrr! It's cold today! A mountain hare shivers as it lies in its shallow form. The form helps protect the hare from the sharp arctic winds. Although its dense, three-layered fur helps trap its body heat, arctic winters are fierce. Even though daytime is resting time, the hare takes only short naps. Every few minutes, it wakes up to groom itself and peer around for signs of danger.

Like snowshoe hares and Arctic hares, mountain hares are well adapted to life in the far north. In late fall, their coats change from brown to gray-white. Their light coat helps camouflage them against the snow, and it also helps keep them warm. When the light reaches the lower layers of fur, it traps warmth next to their skin.

Mountain hares have other ways to protect themselves from the snow and cold. In winter, they gather in groups of twenty or more on the side of a hill where the wind is less fierce. The snow is not as deep here, and the hares can scrape it away with their feet to get to the lichens and mosses underneath. As they feed, the hares turn their backs to the wind.

During the mating season, the males fight over the females. Many males will mate with a single female, but she is the one in control. A female mountain hare is choosy. If she doesn't care for a particular male, she will box at him to drive him away.

Pikas

FAMILY: Ochotonidae
COMMON EXAMPLE: Collared pika
GENUS AND SPECIES: *Ochotona collaris*
SIZE: 7 to 7 3/4 inches (18 to 20 cm)

At first glance, you might confuse a collared pika with an American pika. Both are gray and about the same size. But a collared pika has a "collar" of creamy fur on its neck and shoulders, and this species lives in the mountains of Alaska and northwestern Canada.

Like American pikas, collared pikas start building haypiles in late summer. They need to have extra food for the hard winter ahead. Each pika makes several haypiles in its territory and defends them from intruders. Year after year, it usually builds its piles in the same places under overhanging rocks. Sometimes a pika may eat up all its stores. Then it has to feed on lichen and cushion plants by tunneling under the snow.

Unlike many lagomorphs, collared pikas mate for life. Compared to rabbits and hares, pikas don't produce a lot of young. Each female has just two litters a year with about three babies at a time. The young are tiny, blind, and helpless, but they grow fast. They can

32

reach adult size in only 40 days. Even though they have so few young, collared pikas are plentiful in Alaska. This is probably because they live in remote areas where people don't bother them.

Collared pikas have many ways to talk to one another. They bleat like little sheep, bark like tiny dogs, and call out "Yink! Yink! Enk!" During the mating season, the males click their teeth and chatter at the females. What noisy lagomorphs!

Rabbits

FAMILY: Leporidae
EXAMPLE: Marsh rabbit
GENUS AND SPECIES: *Sylvilagus palustris*
SIZE: 13 1/2 to 17 1/2 inches (35 to 45 cm)

A swamp is the last place you would expect to see a rabbit, but marsh rabbits don't seem to know that. They build mazes of runways through the swamp grasses and follow them to find the leaves, shoots, buds, and flowers they love. A marsh rabbit normally walks instead of hopping like most rabbits. But when it spots an enemy, it hops away in a zigzag pattern and dives into the water. A marsh rabbit is a good swimmer, and it can hide underwater for several minutes. Its enemy usually gives up and trots away.

Marsh rabbits have a lot of enemies—from foxes to hawks—and most of these lagomorphs don't live past their first year. They have a lot of young so that some may survive. They breed almost year round and produce as many as six litters every year. A litter usually contains about six young, but sometimes as many as fifteen kittens are born at one time.

At mating times, the male marsh rabbits seem to go crazy. They run about after the females as they vie for their attention. They fight fiercely among themselves over the females, until the strongest male wins and gets to mate with a female. Then they start again.

After she mates, a female marsh rabbit makes her nest. She builds a platform of rushes to keep the nest dry, then makes a den that she lines with fur from her chest. Even in the swamp, the kittens will be warm and dry.

Marsh rabbits are endangered. As the human population grows, people have been draining the swamps and building houses and factories where the rabbits once lived. Unless their habitat is protected, marsh rabbits may disappear forever.

Cottontails

FAMILY: Leporidae
COMMON EXAMPLE: Desert cottontail
GENUS AND SPECIES: *Sylvilagus audubonii*
SIZE: 16 inches (41 cm)

Desert cottontails live in dry plains—where there is not much to eat. Still, these cottontails manage to survive. They nibble on grasses or on mesquite pods. They can even eat prickly pear pads.

Desert cottontails come out in the evening to feed. During the day, they hide from their many enemies in heavy brush or brambles. If a coyote smells a cottontail, it will freeze. It blends in with its surroundings, so the coyote may not see it.

If its enemy does spot it, the cottontail darts away and flicks its puffy white tail. Like other cottontails, it runs in a zigzag pattern as it races for safety. It can also swim and climb up a tree or a brush-pile to escape.

A female desert cottontail raises about five litters a year. She digs a shallow hole in the ground and lines it with soft grass and fur she plucks from her chest. The blind, helpless kittens hide in the nest, and their mother feeds them only three times a night. She stays away from the nest the rest of the time. Hungry coyotes are less likely to find the kittens if she leaves them alone.

Jack Rabbits

FAMILY: Leporidae
COMMON EXAMPLE: Black-tailed jack rabbit
GENUS AND SPECIES: *Lepus californicus*
SIZE: 18 to 24 1/2 inches (46 to 62 cm)

Can you guess how the jack rabbit got its name? Its long ears reminded the early Europeans of a donkey's ears, so they called it the "jackass rabbit." The name was later shortened to "jack rabbit." Jack rabbits aren't really rabbits, though. They are hares.

A black-tailed jack rabbit's long ears help it survive. It is found throughout much of the western United States, and it often lives in dry desert areas. When it's very hot, a jack rabbit raises its ears to let off heat through its big ear surfaces. In the cold winter, it keeps its ears pressed flat on its body to prevent heat loss.

Jack rabbits are well adapted to life in the desert. In the summer, they find grass and other plants to eat. In the winter, they eat twigs and bark. They will also eat cactus if they have to. They nibble on the soft parts until nothing is left but the spines. They don't need much water, either. They get most of the water they need from the plants they eat.

When an enemy startles a jack rabbit, it will freeze. If that trick doesn't work, it will spring away 20 feet (6 m) at a bound and zigzag off at up to 35 mph (56 kph). The long-legged black-tailed jack rabbit is the fastest of all the hares.

Rabbits

FAMILY: Leporidae
EXAMPLE: Bushman rabbit
GENUS AND SPECIES: *Bunolagus monticularis*
SIZE: 13 to 18 inches (33 to 46 cm)

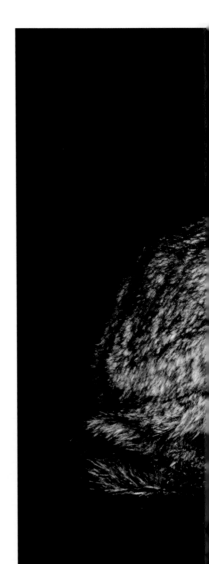

Bushman rabbits live only in the thick bushes around rivers in the Karoo highlands of South Africa, but there are hardly any of them left. These rabbits were first discovered in 1902. Then they were not seen for many years afterward. In 1929, a man named C. G. Shortridge went to South Africa to find them. He wanted to add them to his museum collection.

People told him to search in the mountain cliffs. He spent 18 years trying to find them with no luck. He finally came across a small group of bushman rabbits hiding in the scrub along a riverbank—not where he expected to find them! He captured four of them for his museum.

It would be another 31 years before another bushman rabbit was captured. These shy creatures are so rare that scientists don't know much about them. Mr. Shortridge wrote, "Bushman [rabbits] move slowly and awkwardly, like newborn lambs.

Their tails hang down between their hind legs. They run so slowly that any dog would be able to catch them."

If that is so, it may explain why they are so rare. (The photograph on this page shows a stuffed bushman rabbit.) We may never learn more about them before they vanish from Earth.

Lagomorphs and People

Rabbits make good pets.

People have been hunting rabbits and hares for thousands of years. They eat the meat and use the fur to make coats or to line gloves. They also use the fur to make felt for hats.

About a thousand years ago, French monks started taming wild European rabbits so they wouldn't have to hunt to have meat. They created many different breeds in a variety of sizes and colors.

Over the years, people have continued to raise and breed rabbits. Now there are more than fifty different breeds. These days, most rabbits are kept as pets instead of for meat. All of them, from the long-haired angora rabbit to the lop-eared rabbit, descended from the wild European rabbit.

People enjoyed rabbit meat so much that they brought rabbits into places where they never lived before, such as South America, New Zealand, and Australia. But sometimes this backfired. In Australia, the rabbits multiplied rapidly because they had no natural predators. Now they have become serious pests. They eat crops and grasslands that people want to keep for themselves and their livestock. Getting rid of them is much harder than getting them there in the first place!

Other lagomorphs are having a difficult time surviving. Many, such as volcano rabbits, bushman rabbits, and marsh rabbits, are threatened or endangered species. Sometimes they are in trouble because of overhunting by people or their dogs. More often, it is because people are destroying their habitats.

Today there are organizations trying to protect these species. But it is an uphill fight. Their habitats are still being destroyed, and people still hunt them illegally. How sad if these fascinating animals become extinct!

When people build new houses, they destroy the habitats of many animals.

Words to Know

buck—a male rabbit

burrow—a shelter dug in the ground

cheek teeth—a lagomorph's back teeth used to chew food

class—a group of creatures within a phylum that share certain characteristics

colony—a group of animals that live together and work as a single unit

den—the shelter or resting place of a wild animal

doe—a female rabbit

family—a group of creatures within an order that share certain characteristics

form—a shallow hollow where a hare makes its nest

genus (plural **genera**)—a group of creatures within a family that share certain characteristics

habitat—the natural environment where an animal lives and grows

herbivore—an animal that eats only plants

incisor—a front tooth used for gnawing and cutting

kingdom—one of the five divisions into which all living things are placed: the animal kingdom, the plant kingdom, the fungus kingdom, the moneran kingdom, and the protist kingdom

kitten—the name for a baby rabbit

lagomorph—the name for the order of small mammals that includes rabbits, pikas, and hares

leveret—the name for a baby hare

order—a group of creatures within a class that share certain characteristics

phylum (plural **phyla**)—a group of creatures within a kingdom that share certain characteristics

predator—an animal that hunts and eats other animals

species—a group of creatures within a genus that share certain characteristics. Members of a species can mate and produce young

territory—the area where an animal lives, hunts, and has young

Learning More

Books

Barkhausen, Annette and Frank Geiser. *Rabbits and Hares.* Milwaukee, WI: Gareth Stevens, 1994.

Boring, Mel. *Rabbits, Squirrels, and Chipmunks.* Minoqua, WI: Northword Press, 1996.

Fisher, Ron. *Cottontails: Little Rabbits of Field and Forest.* Washington, D.C.: National Geographic Society, 1997.

Kitchen, Bert. *The Rabbit.* New York: Kingfisher, 2000.

Nickles, Greg. *Pikas.* Danbury, CT: Grolier Educational, 2001.

Zeaman, John. *From Pests to Pets: How Small Mammals Became Our Friends.* Danbury, CT: Franklin Watts, 1998.

Web Sites

The Animal Diversity Web

http://animaldiversity.ummz.umich.edu/index.html

Search this site for information on members of the animal kingdom. There are more than seventeen detailed descriptions of lagomorphs.

House Rabbit Society

http://www.rabbit.org/

If you have a pet rabbit or would like to get one, this site can give you information about caring for rabbits.

Index

About the Author

Sara Swan Miller has enjoyed working with children all her life, first as a Montessori nursery school teacher, and later as an outdoor environmental educator at the Mohonk Preserve in New Paltz, New York. As director of the school program, she has led hundreds of schoolchildren on field trips and taught them the importance of appreciating and respecting the natural world.

She has written a number of children's books, including *Three Stories You Can Read to Your Dog*; *Three Stories You Can Read to Your Cat*; *Three More Stories You Can Read to Your Dog*; *Three More Stories You Can Read to Your Cat*; *What's in the Woods?: An Outdoor Activity Book*; *Oh, Cats of Camp Rabbitbone*; *Piggy in the Parlor and Other Tales*; *Better than TV*; and *Will You Sting Me? Will You Bite?: The Truth About Some Scary-Looking Insects*. She has also written several books on farm animals for Children's Press's True Books series, five books on animal "misfits" for Franklin Watts, and several other books in the Animals in Order series.